Pupil Book 5

Comprehension Skills

Author: Abigail Steel

HarperCollins PUBLISHERS
200
Since 1817

William Collins' dream of knowledge for all began with the publication of his first book in 1819.

A self-educated mill worker, he not only enriched millions of lives, but also founded a flourishing publishing house. Today, staying true to this spirit, Collins books are packed with inspiration, innovation and practical expertise. They place you at the centre of a world of possibility and give you exactly what you need to explore it.

Collins. Freedom to teach.

Published by Collins
An imprint of HarperCollins*Publishers*
The News Building
1 London Bridge Street
London
SE1 9GF

Browse the complete Collins catalogue at
www.collins.co.uk

© HarperCollins*Publishers* Limited 2017

10 9 8 7 6 5 4 3 2 1

ISBN 978-0-00-823638-0

British Library Cataloguing in Publication Data

A Catalogue record for this publication is available from the British Library

Publishing Director: Lee Newman
Publishing Manager: Helen Doran
Senior Editor: Hannah Dove
Project Manager: Emily Hooton
Author: Abigail Steel
Development Editor: Hannah Hirst-Dunton
Copy-editor: Ros & Chris Davies
Proofreader: Tracy Thomas
Cover design and artwork: Amparo Barrera and Ken Vail Graphic Design
Internal design concept: Amparo Barrera
Typesetter: Jouve India Private Ltd
Illustrations: Beatriz Castro, Dante Ginevra, Andres Avaray, Adrian Bijloo, Aptara and QBS
Production Controller: Rachel Weaver

Printed and bound by Grafica Veneta SpA

Acknowledgements

The publishers wish to thank the following for permission to reproduce content. Every effort has been made to trace copyright holders and to obtain their permission for the use of copyright materials. The publishers will gladly receive any information enabling them to rectify any error or omission at the first opportunity.

David Higham Associates Ltd for an extract on page 7 from *The Chicken Gave it to Me* by Anne Fine, Egmont, 2007. Reproduced by permission of David Higham Associates Ltd; Lord Alfred Douglas Literary Estate for the poem on page 16 "The Shark" by Lord Alfred Douglas, copyright © Literary Executors of the Estate of Lord Alfred Douglas. All rights reserved; David Higham Associates Limited for the poem on page 19 "Colonel Fazackerley" by Charles Causley, from *Collected Poems for Children*, Macmillan Children's Books, 2008. Reproduced by permission of David Higham Associates Ltd; Aitken Alexander Associates Ltd for an extract on page 27 from *The Borrowers* by Mary Norton, first published by J.M. Dent and Sons Ltd, copyright © Mary Norton. Reproduced with permission from Aitken Alexander Associates Ltd; and HarperCollins Publishers Ltd for an extract on page 30 from *The Lost Gardens* by Philip Osment, copyright © 2011, Philip Osment. Reproduced by permission of HarperCollins Publishers Ltd; HarperCollins Publishers Ltd for the extract on page 48 from *Your Brain* by Sally Morgan, copyright © 2013 HarperCollins Publishers Ltd; for the extract on page 53-54 from *The Hedgehog Mystery* by Ally Kennen, copyright © 2011 Ally Kennen; for the extract on page 56-57 from *The Dragon Pearl* by Dawn Casey, copyright © Dawn Casey 2015; for the extracts on page 59-60 'What on Earth?' and 'Progress Man!' from *Caliban's Cave* by Judith Nicholls, copyright © 2011 Judith Nicholls; for the extract on page 62-63 from *How to be an Ancient Greek in 25 easy stages* by Scoular Anderson, copyright © 2008 Scoular Anderson; for the extract on page 65 from *Ade Adepitan: A Paralympian's Story* by Ade Adepitan, copyright © HarperCollinsPublishers Limited 2013; for the extracts on page 68 'Summer Afternoon' and 'Gathering in the Days' from *Gathering in the Days* by Gareth Owen, copyright © 2011 Gareth Owen. Reproduced by permission of HarperCollins Publishers Ltd.

p.48 (t) © Masterfile Royalty-Free, p.48 (b) Siri Stafford/Getty Images, p. 50 Scott Olsen/Getty Images, p. 51 Rick Glase/epa/Corbis, p.65 George S de Blonsky/Alamy.

MIX
Paper from responsible sources
FSC™ C007454
FSC
www.fsc.org

This book is produced from independently certified FSC paper to ensure responsible forest management.

For more information visit: **www.harpercollins.co.uk/green**

Contents

Fiction: 'A Clever Way to Catch a Thief'

This is an old tale about a rich man who finds that he is constantly losing things from his house. He suspects that one of his servants may be stealing, but which servant, and how can he be sure to catch the thief?

A Clever Way to Catch a Thief

One evening, when it was getting dark and the servants had finished their day's work, the rich man brought them all together.

"Sadly," he said, "we seem to have a thief amongst us, but with your help I think we can rid ourselves of him or her." The servants looked at each other, sorry to think that one of their number was untrustworthy, but uncertain how the rich man could possibly detect the culprit.

"I have placed a table in the centre of the room next door, and on the table is a box. I have put into the box an old cockerel that possesses magic powers. In turn I want each of you to go into the room. It is dark in there, but don't put on any light. Feel your way to the table and gently rest your left hand on the box."

"But what will that show?" asked one of the servants, quite perplexed.

"If you are not the guilty one, nothing will happen – but if you are the thief, the magic cockerel will immediately detect this and will crow so loudly we shall all immediately hear, and know who is to blame."

The servants glanced at each other, some thinking the rich man might be going mad! Other servants were anxious, not sure whether the cockerel really did possess magic powers. What might happen to them, they thought, if left alone in the dark room with the strange creature?

"If you are innocent you have nothing to fear," reassured the rich man.

So, one by one, the servants went into the room, but not a sound was heard. Not once did the magic cockerel crow.

"Excellent!" exclaimed the rich man as the last servant emerged from the dark room. "Now we know for sure who is the guilty person."

The servants were totally puzzled.

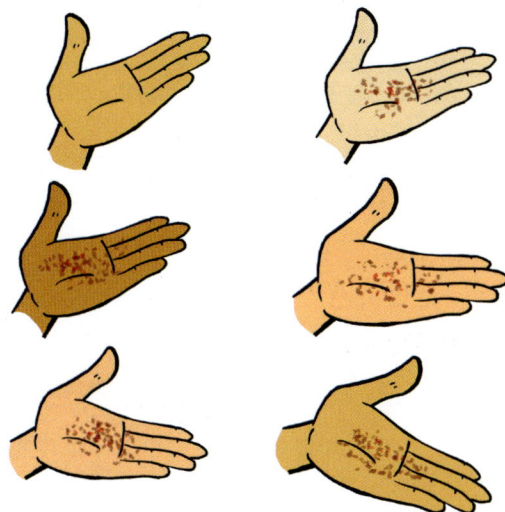

"There is a very good reason why the cockerel made no sound. There was no cockerel in the box to make a sound! Each of you now show me your left hand. There was no cockerel, but there was soot on top of the box," said the man.

"You," he exclaimed, thrusting his finger towards the only servant with a clean hand, "must be the guilty person. You were the only person frightened to place your hand on top of the box!"

Get started

Write sentences to answer each question. Refer to the text in your answer.

1. In your own words, explain the vocabulary below in the context of the story. Use a dictionary for help.

   | perplexed | guilt | innocence | anxious | soot |

2. Why did the rich man think one of his servants had been stealing from him?

3. Why did the innocent servants have nothing to fear?

4. Who had soot on their hands?

5. Why didn't the cockerel make a sound?

6. At what point in the day did the event in the text happen?

7. Which hand of each servant did the rich man want to check?

8. How did the rich man know who the guilty servant was?

Try these

Write sentences to answer each question. Explain how or why you came up with your answer.

1. How do you think the rich man felt when he realised someone was stealing from him?

2. Why do you think the servants were 'sorry to think that one of their number was untrustworthy'?

3. Why do you think the rich man pretended he had a magical cockerel?

4. How do you think the innocent servants felt when they were going into the dark room?

5. How do you think the guilty servant felt when he or she was going into the dark room?

6. Why did some of the servants think the rich man was going mad?

7. What do you think the rich man will or should do, now that he has found the culprit?

8. Is this a historical story?

Now try these

1. Write notes about the different feelings that the guilty servant would have at different points during the story. When and why would the servant feel these different emotions?

2. Describe the character of the rich man, based on what you learn in the extract.

3. Explain why the moment the rich man says 'Excellent!' is a turning point in the story.

4. Look at this phrase: 'thrusting his finger towards the only servant with a clean hand'. What does this phrase describe? Explain how it is effective.

5. Write a longer ending for the story, using at least ten lines of dialogue between the guilty servant, the innocent servants and the rich man. Then add a moral for the story. Why do you think this is the moral?

Fiction: 'I Go Chicken-Dippy'

From 'The Chicken Gave It to Me' by Anne Fine

I'd never been outside before. Never in my whole life. I went quite silly, really. I feel a bit of a fool even now, thinking back on it. But I went chicken-dippy. I couldn't handle it at all, not everything at once. Not when the only thing I'd known since I was hatched was wire netting and other chickens.

Try and imagine! First, how it felt. All that wet air and wind. I'd never felt wet air ruffling my feathers before. I'd never even been wet. Now here I was staggering about in a slimy mud puddle, stung by fierce little cold raindrops. It was so wonderful! It was like being born again. I felt I'd come alive!

And the noise! Roaring wind. Creaking tree tops. Deafening! The storm sounded like the world cracking in half, just for me, to wake me after a lifetime of having my ears stuffed with chicken cackle. I wanted to do my bit, so I joined in, clucking and squawking like something gone loopy. Being outside in the fresh air was great.

And it was fresh. Fresh and cold. But what I'd never guessed was how many smells go to make up fresh air. Inside the shed was terrible – terrible! Too awful to describe. At the weekends, when we weren't cleaned out, it was even worse. The workers always wore masks, but even so, on some mornings they coughed and choked, and their eyes were red-rimmed. (Imagine how we felt. We'd been in it all night!) Outside, I smelled a thousand things I couldn't even name until later – the leaf-mould underfoot, wet bracken, a thread of exhaust fumes from the road behind, cow parsnip, smoke from the chimney over the hill, the film of oil on the puddles. A giant stew. Smells of the World! And I was breathing it in for the first time. Me – a bedraggled middle-aged feather baby. But I felt good.

Get started

Write sentences to answer each question. Refer to the text in your answer.

1. How many times had the chicken been outside before?

2. What was the first thing the chicken felt outside?

3. What did the wet air do to the chicken's feathers?

4. In what was the chicken staggering about?

5. What was the temperature like outside?

6. What could the chicken hear outside?

7. When was the chicken shed cleaned out?

8. What did the workers look like?

Try these

Write sentences to answer each question. Explain how or why you came up with your answer.

1. Would the chicken prefer to be in the shelter of the chicken shed or outside in the storm?

2. Why do you think the workers in the shed wore masks?

3. Why couldn't the chicken name the things it smelled until later?

4. Why do you think the chicken had never been outside before?

5. Why do you think the chicken felt it 'couldn't handle it all'?

6. What do you think 'chicken-dippy' means?

7. Why do you think the chickens were kept in sheds in the way they were?

8. Do you think this is a good reason for using chicken sheds like the one described in the extract?

Now try these

1. Describe the character of the chicken, based on what you learn in the extract.

2. Make a mind map about the different feelings that the chicken would have at different points during the story, including when it was still in the shed. Think about when and why the chicken would feel these different emotions.

3. What different senses has the author used to describe the chicken's feelings? What effect does using these senses have on you as a reader?

4. Look at this section again: 'And the noise! Roaring wind. Creaking tree tops. Deafening!'

   The author has used short fragments that are not full sentences. Why do you think she has done this? What effect does it have?

5. Write the next part of the story. What will the chicken do? What other senses could you describe?

Fiction (classic): 'Robinson Crusoe'

From 'Robinson Crusoe' by Daniel Defoe

Robinson Crusoe has been shipwrecked on a remote island.

Eighth day   Yesterday I brought back from the ship a quantity of tools, a drill, a dozen hatchets, a grind-stone for sharpening, iron crowbars, a large bag of nails and rivets; with sails, ropes, poles, two barrels of powder, a box of musket balls, seven muskets, a third shotgun, lead, a hammock, a mattress, blankets, clothes and great coats. I thought that I had rescued nearly everything that was on board. But I was wrong, for today, returning from a trip to the wreck that almost cost me dear – the wind having risen, I capsized with my whole load in the middle of the creek – I saw Japp, the captain's dog, come bounding joyfully along, an Irish setter I had thought drowned with the crew. I think that the poor beast, swept away by the current had landed on the island much farther away, and had difficulty in finding me. This evening I pitched a little tent with the poles and sail-cloth, under which I spread my bed. I have piled up all my riches in a shelter from the rain that was threatening. My dog snores at my feet, I have dined on a bit of dried meat and a ship's biscuit, and in spite of a rising wind I am prepared to pass a good night.

Get started

Write sentences to answer each question. Refer to the text in your answer.

1. For how many days has Robinson Crusoe been shipwrecked?

2. What surprised Crusoe on the eighth day?

3. What type of dog was Japp?

4. Who had been Japp's master?

5. Why did Crusoe think it had been difficult for Japp to find him?

6. What did Crusoe do with the poles and sail-cloth?

7. What did Crusoe eat for dinner?

8. List five items that Crusoe recovered from the shipwreck.

Try these

Write sentences to answer each question. Explain how or why you came up with your answer.

1. Crusoe says his trip 'almost cost me dear'. What does he mean by this? What is Crusoe concerned about, and why?

2. How do you think Japp felt about Crusoe?

3. How do you think Crusoe felt about Japp?

4. How was Crusoe feeling by the end of the day?

5. Why do you think Crusoe ate so little dinner?

6. Why do you think Crusoe wants to save the tools from the ship?

7. Why do you think Crusoe is writing a diary?

8. Is this a historical story?

Now try these

1. Describe the character of Robinson Crusoe, based on what you learn in the extract.

2. Make a mind map about the different feelings that Crusoe would have had at different points during the story, including before and during the shipwreck. Think about when and why he would feel these different emotions.

3. Note down at least three features that tell you the extract is a diary entry.

4. Look at the very long sentence that starts with 'But I was wrong'. Note down the three events reported in the sentence. Why do you think Crusoe uses long, complicated sentences instead of short, snappy ones? What effect do they have?

5. Write a letter from Robinson Crusoe to his family. Think carefully about what he would want to tell them, and what he may not want to say.

Non-fiction (news report): 'Cubs and Brownies to the rescue'

LATEST NEWS

MORETON Weekly

4 August

Cubs and Brownies to the RESCUE

MORETON: Anglers and conservation volunteers were joined yesterday by Cubs and Brownies from packs in the town to help with the annual spring clean of Prospect Park as part of the RESCUE event.

Moreton Town Council and Friends of Caversham Woods backed the local rivers and environmental clean-up event, along with other local authorities and voluntary groups.

The good news for those taking part was that the volume of rubbish was less than previous years, and down by about half on three years ago when the scheme was launched.

"However, there are still a few local residents who are dumping garden and other refuse within the park," according to a spokeswoman for the environment department at the council. "Recently a large amount of old engine oil was illegally disposed of in a litter bin, which could have caused a pollution accident."

The town's mayor, Mr Jack Alaman, who watched the working parties in the park, commented, "The majority of visitors to our park are proud of our town and its park. They do not leave litter or dump rubbish. But you always seem to get a few who spoil it for the many. I am pleased to see so many young people here to help clean up the park. We seek to involve local schools and youth groups in the care of the area, in the hope that the next generation will care for their environment."

Get started

Write sentences to answer each question. Refer to the news report in your answer.

1. In your own words, explain the vocabulary below in the context of the report. Use a dictionary for help.

    | angler | voluntary | scheme | launch | refuse | dispose |

2. Who was involved in the clean-up?

3. How often does the clean-up happen?

4. What date did the clean-up happen this year?

5. How long ago was the scheme launched?

6. How much more rubbish was there in the first year, compared to the year the report was written?

7. Who is still dumping garden refuse in the park?

8. Why was it wrong to leave engine oil in a litter bin? Give both reasons.

Try these

Write sentences to answer each question. Explain how or why you came up with your answer.

1. Why do you think the Cubs and Brownies were helping with the clean-up?

2. How do you think the Cubs and Brownies felt about being involved with the clean-up event?

3. Why do you think someone might dump rubbish in a park?

4. What effect do you think this rubbish has on the park?

5. How do you think the spokeswoman for the environment department felt about the issue?

6. What was the main feeling that the mayor expressed about the clean-up?

7. Why might newspaper readers want to read about this story?

8. What effect might the report have on the people who dump rubbish in the park?

Now try these

1. Describe what the RESCUE event is, based on what you learn from the report.

2. Note down at least three features that tell you this is a news report.

3. Why do you think the report uses the two quotations, from the spokeswoman for the environment department and the mayor? What effect do they have on the report?

4. Based on the information in the extract, design a leaflet or poster meant to stop people leaving litter and rubbish in the park.

5. Write a speech for the mayor to read out, to thank everyone involved in the project. Think about what details he would include, how he feels and what kind of language he would use.

Poetry: 'The Shark'

A treacherous monster is the Shark
He never makes the least remark

And when he sees you on the sand,
He doesn't seem to want to land.

He watches you take off your clothes,
And not the least excitement shows.

His eyes do not grow bright or roll,
He has astounding self-control.

He waits till you are quite undressed,
And seems to take no interest.

And when towards the sea you leap,
He looks as if he were asleep.

But when you once get in his range,
His whole demeanour seems to change.

He throws his body right about,
And his true character comes out.

It's no use crying or appealing,
He seems to lose all decent feeling.

After this warning you will wish
To keep clear of this treacherous fish.

His back is black, his stomach white,
He has a very dangerous bite.

Lord Alfred Douglas

Get started

Write sentences to answer each question. Refer to the poem in your answer.

1. In your own words, explain the vocabulary below in the context of the poem. Use a dictionary for help.

   | astounding | range | demeanour | character | appealing |

2. How does the poet describe the shark's eyes?

3. What doesn't the shark do 'when he sees you on the sand'?

4. What doesn't the shark do when he 'watches you take off your clothes'?

5. What does the shark do with his body when his demeanour changes?

6. Does the shark's behaviour change when you first get into the sea?

7. When does the shark's behaviour change?

8. What does the poet believe the reader will wish to do after reading the poem?

Try these

Write sentences to answer each question. Explain how or why you came up with your answer.

1. How does the word 'monster' affect the reader's feelings towards the shark?

2. Why do you think the poet calls the shark 'treacherous'? Use a dictionary for help.

3. What is the shark's 'true character'?

4. Why do you think the shark might pretend 'to take no interest' until you 'get in his range'?

5. Why do you think the poet chose to use rhyming couplets?

6. Do you think the poet feels anything positive about the shark?

7. The poet refers to the shark's lack of 'decent feeling'. What do you think he means by this? Can animals have 'decent feeling'?

8. Find two other things the poet writes about the shark that usually only apply to people.

Now try these

1. Describe the character of the shark, based on what the poet writes in the poem.

2. How do you think the shark might feel about the person getting undressed on the beach and swimming in the sea? Note down a few rhyming couplets from the shark's point of view.

3. Explain why the line that starts with 'But' is a turning point in the poem.

4. 'He throws his body right about' describes something different from the rest of the poem. Explain how it is different.

5. Write a similar poem, in the first person, from the shark's point of view.

Poetry: 'Colonel Fazackerley'

Colonel Fazackerley Butterworth-Toast
Bought an old castle complete with a ghost,
But someone or other forgot to declare
To Colonel Fazack that the spectre was there.

On the very first evening, while waiting to dine,
The Colonel was taking a fine sherry wine,
When the ghost, with a furious flash and a flare,
Shot out of the chimney and shivered, 'Beware!'

Colonel Fazackerley put down his glass
And said, 'My dear fellow, that's really first class!
I just can't conceive how you do it at all.
I imagine you're going to a Fancy Dress Ball?'

At this, the dread ghost gave a withering cry.
Said the Colonel (his monocle firm in his eye),
'Now just how do you do it I wish I could think.
Do sit down and tell me, and please have a drink.'

The ghost in his phosphorous cloak gave a roar
And floated about between ceiling and floor.
He walked through a wall and returned through a pane
And backed up the chimney and came down again.

Said the Colonel, 'With laughter I'm feeling quite weak!'
(As tears of merriment ran down his cheek).
'My house-warming party I hope you won't spurn.
You must say you'll come and you'll give us a turn!'

At this, the poor spectre – quite out of his wits –
Proceeded to shake himself almost to bits.
He rattled his chains and he clattered his bones
And he filled the whole castle with mumbles and moans.

But Colonel Fazackerley, just as before,
Was simply delighted and called out, 'Encore!'
At which the ghost vanished, his efforts in vain,
And was never seen at the castle again.

'Oh dear, what a pity!' said Colonel Fazack.
'I don't know his name, so I can't call him back.'
And then with a smile that was hard to define,
Colonel Fazackerley went in to dine.

Charles Causley

Get started

Write sentences to answer each question. Refer to the text in your answer.

1. What did Colonel Fazackerley buy?

2. What was the Colonel drinking on his first evening in his new home?

3. What did he put down when he first saw the ghost?

4. What did the Colonel call the ghost, when he first met him?

5. When the Colonel invited the ghost to sit down and have a drink, what did the ghost do?

6. Why does the Colonel say he wants the ghost to come to his house-warming party?

7. What did the Colonel call out when he was delighted by the ghost's actions?

8. What did the Colonel do after the ghost disappeared?

Try these

Write sentences to answer each question. Explain how or why you came up with your answer.

1. How would you describe the structure of this poem?

2. Is the ghost friendly? Is the Colonel afraid of the ghost?

3. The Colonel says, 'I imagine you're going to a Fancy Dress Ball'. What does this suggest he thinks the ghost is?

4. Why was the ghost 'quite out of his wits'?

5. What effect did the Colonel's behaviour have on the ghost in the end?

6. Why do you think the Colonel was smiling as he went for dinner?

7. Do you think the Colonel really believed the ghost was 'going to a Fancy Dress Ball'?

8. How do you think the poet feels about the ghost?

Now try these

1. Describe the character of the Colonel, based on what you learn from the extract.

2. Think about the moment that the Colonel first sees the ghost, before he speaks to it. Write notes about what must have gone through his mind as he quickly considers what to do.

3. Write notes about the different thoughts and feelings that the ghost would have at different points during the poem. When and why would the ghost feel these different emotions?

4. The poet says the Colonel's smile is 'hard to define', rather than explaining why the Colonel is smiling. What effect does this have on the end of the poem?

5. Write two more verses for the poem, from the ghost's point of view. How does the ghost feel about what happened, and what might it do now? Use the same verse structure as in the poem.

Non-fiction (formal letter): 'Noisy neighbour'

Environmental Health Department
Southborough Council, High Street, Southborough

Mr J. Trigger
9 Hornsey Lane
Southborough

1 October

Dear Sir,

I fear that we have received yet another complaint from one of your neighbours concerning the noise emanating from your home. This is not the first occasion we have had cause to draw this matter to your attention. I refer to my letters of 29 July and 16 August.

On both occasions you assured me that the problem would cease forthwith, but those promises appear not to have been fulfilled.

The present complaint refers not only to the volume of the music which you, or the other members of your family, are playing from early morning until midnight, but also to the sound of your dogs constantly fighting, musical instruments being played at loud volumes and household appliances, which I'm informed are in use incessantly.

This letter is our final warning before we shall be forced to take further action to restrain your total disregard for the welfare of your neighbours.

Yours faithfully
Mr B. Quiet
Complaints Officer

Get started

Write sentences to answer each question. Refer to the text in your answer.

1. Who wrote the letter? From where did he send it?

2. Who is meant to receive the letter? Where does he live?

3. What is the purpose of the letter?

4. Who made the complaints?

5. What four examples of offensive behaviour are mentioned?

6. Does Mr Trigger live alone?

7. When did Mr Quiet first write to Mr Trigger?

8. How many times in total has Mr Quiet written to Mr Trigger? How many times has Mr Trigger replied to Mr Quiet?

Try these

Write sentences to answer each question. Explain how or why you came up with your answer.

1. What do you think Mr Trigger's neighbour wanted to happen when he complained?

2. Why do you think Mr Quiet is writing this letter instead of the neighbour himself?

3. Why do you think Mr Trigger has not reduced his noise, despite two previous letters being sent?

4. What do you think 'further action' might mean?

5. Do you think this will be an effective letter?

6. How do you think Mr Trigger's neighbour feels, after all this time?

7. How do you think Mr Quiet feels about sending this letter?

8. How do you think Mr Trigger will feel about receiving this letter?

Now try these

1. Describe the character of Mr Trigger, based on what you learn in the extract.

2. Note down at least three features that tell you the extract is a letter.

3. The letter uses formal language. Choose less formal words or phrases that could be swapped for the vocabulary below. Use a dictionary for help.

| emanating | occasion | forthwith | fulfilled | incessantly | restrain | disregard |

4. How do you think the effect of the letter would change if it used informal language?

5. Write a reply to this letter from Mr J. Trigger. What might he and his family think about the complaints? Will he use formal language, too?

Fiction (classic): 'Pinocchio'

From 'Pinocchio' by Michael and Clare Morpurgo

Chapter One

My name's Pinocchio and this is my story. It all began one evening when Gepetto, my father, who was a woodcutter, came home and said to his wife, "Look what I've made. I've made us our own little boy. The little boy we've always wanted."

And that was me, Pinocchio!

My mother was so happy. She hugged me to her and then she hugged Gepetto and we all danced round the room together! However, I quickly learnt that not everyone thought I was so wonderful. In the street they called me Wobbly-Head, Wooden-Top, Clumpy-Feet, and I didn't like that at all. So I ran away.

How I could run! I ran in leaps and bounds, tickety tackety, down the cobbled street. I dodged this way and that until Signor Biffo, the big policeman, caught me and took me home to Mama and Papa.

"Please never run away again, Pinocchio," said Mama, hugging me to her.

"Tomorrow you'll go to school," said Papa. "You'll like it there and you'll make lots of friends."

But I didn't like it there at all and I didn't make lots of friends. So, although I loved Mama and Papa, I decided to run away again and see the world and make my fortune.

Chapter Two

Once again I ran in leaps and bounds, tickety tackety, down the cobbled street and out into the countryside.
Soon it started to rain and I began to feel cold and hungry. So when I saw a little cottage with the door standing open, I went in. Imagine how pleased I was to find some bread on the table and a warm fire crackling in the hearth. Lickety split, I ate the bread and curled up by the fire to warm myself.

Then I heard a little voice. "Cri-cri," it went, and I saw a tiny cricket crawling up the wall beside me. To my surprise he said, "Running away is always a foolish idea. It never makes you happy and it makes your Mama and Papa very sad."

Get started

Write sentences to answer each question. Refer to the text in your answer.

1. What was Gepetto's job?
2. What names did Pinocchio get called?
3. How did Pinocchio feel about school?
4. Why did Pinocchio decide to run away on each occasion?
5. Why did Pinocchio go into the little cottage?
6. What did Pinocchio do inside the cottage?
7. Who did Pinocchio meet inside the cottage?
8. What did the cricket tell Pinocchio about running away?

Try these

Write sentences to answer each question. Explain how or why you came up with your answer.

1. Why do you think Gepetto created Pinocchio?
2. Why do you think people in the street called Pinocchio names?
3. How do you think Gepetto and his wife felt when Pinocchio kept running away?
4. How do you think Pinocchio felt about running away?
5. Why might Pinocchio have thought it was acceptable to let himself into the little cottage?
6. What do you think is the cricket's opinion of Pinocchio?
7. Why do you think the author repeats the phrase 'I ran in leaps and bounds, tickety tackety, down the cobbled street'?
8. Who is narrating the story?

Now try these

1. Write notes about the different emotions that Pinocchio would have felt at different points during the story. When and why would Pinocchio feel these different emotions?
2. Describe the character of Pinocchio, based on what you learn in the extract.
3. Look at this section again: 'Lickety split, I ate the bread and curled up by the fire to warm myself.'

   How is this sentence effective in showing Pinocchio to be impulsive and thoughtless?
4. Write a letter from Pinocchio to his parents. Think carefully about what he would want to tell them and what he may not want to say.
5. Write the next part of the story. What will Pinocchio do? Who else will he meet?

Fiction (classic): 'The Borrowers'

From 'The Borrowers' by Mary Norton

Kate had sometimes wondered what happens to the little things that go missing. In this extract Mrs May tells her about the Borrowers, tiny people who live in the homes of humans, and borrow what they need to survive.

"I've lost the crochet hook …" (they were making a bed-quilt – in woollen squares; there were thirty still to do), "I know where I put it," she went on hastily; "I put it on the bottom shelf of the book-case just beside my bed."

"On the bottom shelf?" repeated Mrs May, her own needle flicking steadily in the firelight. "Near the floor?"

"Yes," said Kate, "But I looked on the floor. Under the rug. Everywhere. The wool was still there though. Just where I'd left it."

"Oh dear," exclaimed Mrs May lightly, "don't say they're in this house too!"

"That what are?" asked Kate.

"The Borrowers," said Mrs May, and in the half light she seemed to smile.

Kate stared a little fearfully. "Are there such things?" she asked after a moment.

"As what?"

Kate blinked her eyelids. "As people, other people, living in a house who … borrow things?"

Mrs May laid down her work. "What do you think?" she asked.

"I don't know," said Kate looking away and pulling hard at her shoe button. "There can't be. And yet" – she raised her head – "and yet sometimes I think there must be."

"Why do you think there must be?" asked Mrs May.

"Because of all the things that disappear. Safety pins, for instance. Factories go on making safety pins, and every day people go on buying safety pins and yet, somehow, there is never a safety pin just when you want one. Where are they all? Now, at this minute? Where do they all go? Take needles," she went on. "All the needles my mother ever bought – there must be hundreds – can't just be lying around this house."

"Not lying about this house, no," agreed Mrs May.

"And all the other things we keep on buying. Again and again and again. Like pencils and match boxes and sealing wax and hair slides and drawing pins and thimbles –"

"And hatpins," put in Mrs May, "and blotting paper."

"Yes, blotting paper," agreed Kate, "but not hatpins."

"That's where you're wrong," said Mrs May, and she picked up her work again. "There was a reason for hatpins."

Kate stared. "A reason?" she repeated. "I mean – what kind of a reason?"

"Well, there are two reasons really. A hatpin is a very useful weapon and" – Mrs May laughed suddenly – "but it all sounds such nonsense and" – she hesitated – "it was so very long ago!"

"But tell me" said Kate, "tell me how you know about the hatpin. Did you ever see one?"

Mrs May threw her a startled glance. "Well, yes –" she began.

"Not a hatpin," exclaimed Kate impatiently, "a – what-ever-do-you-call-them, a Borrower?"

Mrs May drew a sharp breath. "No," she said quickly, "I never saw one."

"But someone else saw one," cried Kate, "and you know about it. I can see you do!"

"Hush," said Mrs May, "no need to shout!" She gazed downwards at the upturned face and then she smiled and her eyes slid away into the distance.

Get started

Write sentences to answer each question. Refer to the text in your answer.

1. In your own words, explain the vocabulary below in the context of the story. Use a dictionary for help.

   | crochet | quilt | hastily | thimble | hesitated | startled |

2. What had Kate lost?

3. How many woollen squares did she still need to make?

4. Where did Kate put the item she had now lost?

5. Where did she look for it?

6. Give three examples of other items that Kate thinks often go missing.

7. Who did Mrs May think was responsible for the missing items?

8. Has Mrs May ever seen a Borrower?

Try these

Write sentences to answer each question. Explain how or why you came up with your answer.

1. What have all the lost items in common? What does this suggest about the Borrowers?

2. Based on what you learn about the Borrowers, what do you think Mrs May means when she says, 'Not lying about this house, no'?

3. Why do you think Mrs May laughs suddenly?

4. Why do you think Mrs May draws a sharp breath?

5. Why do you think Mrs May's 'eyes slid away into the distance'?

6. Why do you think Kate raised her voice at the end of the extract?

7. How do you think Kate and Mrs May each feel about Borrowers?

8. Who do you think Mrs May is to Kate? A housekeeper? A nanny?

Now try these

1. Write a list of household items that are small for humans, and then make notes to show how Borrowers might use those items.

2. Describe the character of Kate, based on the extract.

3. Write down all the phrases that describe how Mrs May acts in the extract.

4. Look at the phrases you have just written down. Write notes about the different feelings that Mrs May has at different points in the story. When and why does she feel these different emotions?

5. Imagine a Borrower overhears this conversation. Write the dialogue between this Borrower and their family about what Kate and Mrs May discussed.

Playscript: 'The Lost Gardens'

From 'The Lost Gardens' by Phil Osment

This play is set in a restored garden at the beginning of the 21st century, and then in the same garden at the beginning of the 20th century.

SCENE 1

(An Old Lady sits sleeping in a wheelchair.)
(Sound effect: birds singing)

MAYA	(offstage) Jack! Through here.
JACK	(offstage) Where are you?
MAYA	(offstage) Over here.

(Maya enters and sees the Old Lady.)

OLD LADY	(waking) Ahhhh! There you are at last.
MAYA	Pardon?
OLD LADY	I've been waiting for you. Where are your friends? Jack and Emmy? Do you like the gardens? You know in the old days there were plants from all over the world here? People used to come especially to look at them.
MAYA	Yes, Miss Dickinson told us.
OLD LADY	But then the gardeners left and the family who owned the house moved away and the gardens were forgotten.

(Jack enters holding a map of the gardens.)

JACK	I think we've lost her.
OLD LADY	Ah, there you are, Jack.

(Jack looks up, surprised.)

MAYA	How do you know our names?
OLD LADY	I know everything. You're here with your school to look at the lost gardens. Now isn't it time you went and found the tropical garden?
JACK	What tropical garden?
OLD LADY	It's through there.
JACK	It's not on the map.
OLD LADY	That's because it hasn't been found yet.

(Emmy enters.)

EMMY	You're in trouble. We're not supposed to go off on our own.
OLD LADY	Ah, here she is.
EMMY	Who's she?

(The other two shrug.)

EMMY	She must live in the big house. It's a home for old people. Miss Dickinson said. She looks ancient.

MAYA	That's rude.
OLD LADY	That's all right, my dear. You're having a difficult time at the moment, aren't you, Emmy? Anyway I am ancient. It's true. Now the tropical garden's waiting for you. It's just the other side of the brambles. It used to be called the jungle.
EMMY	Cool.
JACK	It's not on the map.
OLD LADY	Where's your spirit of adventure? Now, you'll need this. There's a gate.

(She hands Jack a huge rusty key.)

OLD LADY	Go on. Take it.

(Jack takes it.)

OLD LADY	It's that way.
JACK	Thanks. Come on, Maya.
MAYA	Goodbye.

(Jack and Maya start to go.)

OLD LADY	But you can't leave without Emmy.
JACK	Oh … well …
OLD LADY	Yes?
MAYA	She doesn't really like the same games as us.
EMMY	Yes I do.
OLD LADY	Take her with you.
EMMY	I don't want to spoil their fun.
OLD LADY	You have to stay together.

(Jack looks at Maya. She shrugs.)

JACK	OK. Come on, Emmy.
OLD LADY	Goodbye, my dears. Be careful of the brambles.

(They go. The Old Lady sleeps.)

Get started

Write sentences to answer each question. Refer to the playscript in your answer.

1. Who are the characters in the play?
2. Where is the play set?
3. Why did people visit the gardens in the past?
4. What is the name of the children's teacher?
5. Why are the children at the gardens?
6. What is Jack holding?
7. How does Emmy describe the Old Lady?
8. What does the Old Lady give Jack?

Try these

Write sentences to answer each question. Explain how or why you came up with your answer.

1. What is the relationship like between the three children?

2. Why do you think Jack and Maya might feel as they do about Emmy?

3. How does the Old Lady react to this relationship?

4. Why do you think she reacts like this?

5. Is Emmy rude to the Old Lady?

6. What do you think the Old Lady might mean when she says that Emmy is 'having a difficult time at the moment'?

7. How do you think the Old Lady knows the children's names?

8. Why do you think the tropical garden 'hasn't been found yet'?

Now try these

1. When Maya appears for the first time, the Old Lady says, 'There you are at last … I've been waiting for you. Where are your friends? Jack and Emmy?'

   What effect do these words have on Maya? What effect do they have on you as a reader?

2. Imagine talking to the Old Lady. Plan six questions to ask her. What would you like to find out to understand the mystery better?

3. Write notes on the things you learn about Emmy from the extract. Then write a short diary entry as Emmy. How do you feel about Jack and Maya? Can you explain the 'difficult time' the Old Lady knows you're having?

4. Imagine you are going to perform the play. Write notes and draw pictures to show the setting, props and costumes you might need to use. Think about your characters carefully when you plan their costumes.

5. Rewrite the extract as a chapter from a story instead of a playscript. How will you explain and describe what is happening?

Poetry: 'A Smuggler's Song'

If you wake at midnight and hear a horse's feet,
Don't go drawing back the blind, or looking at the street,
Them that ask no questions isn't told a lie.
Watch the wall, my darling, while the Gentlemen go by!
    Five and twenty ponies,
    Trotting through the dark –
    Brandy for the Parson,
    'Baccy for the Clerk;
    Laces for the lady; letters for a spy,
And watch the wall, my darling, while the Gentlemen go by!

Running round the woodlump if you chance to find
Little barrels, roped and tarred, all full of brandy-wine;
Don't you shout to come and look, nor take 'em for your play.
Put the brushwood back again – and they'll be gone next day!

If you see the stable-door setting wide open;
If you see a tired horse lying down inside;
If your mother mends a coat cut about and tore;
If the lining's wet and warm – don't you ask no more!

If you meet King George's men, dressed in blue and red,
You be careful what you say, and mindful what is said.
If they call you 'pretty maid', and chuck you 'neath the chin,
Don't you tell where no one is, nor yet where no one's been!

Knocks and footsteps round the house – whistles after dark –
You've no call for running out till the house-dogs bark.
Trusty's here and Pincher's here, and see how dumb they lie –
They don't fret to follow when the Gentlemen go by!

If you do as you've been told, likely there's a chance,
You'll be given a dainty doll, all the way from France,
With a cap of Valenciennes, and a velvet hood –
A present from the Gentlemen, along o' being good!
    Five and twenty ponies,
    Trotting through the dark –
    Brandy for the Parson,
    'Baccy for the Clerk.
Them that asks no questions isn't told a lie –
Watch the wall, my darling, while the
Gentlemen go by!

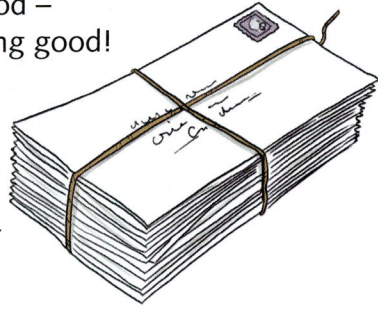

Rudyard Kipling

Get started

Write sentences to answer each question. Refer to the poem in your answer.

1. In your own words, try to explain the vocabulary below in the context of the poem. Use a dictionary or the internet for help, or discuss the words with an adult.

smuggler	'baccy	woodlump	tar	brushwood
mindful	chuck	Valenciennes		

2. At what time should the poem's listener not look out of the window?

3. What were the smugglers bringing for the Parson?

4. Who was getting the laces the smugglers brought?

5. What might the listener see through the open stable door?

6. Who is dressed in red and blue?

7. Who are 'Trusty' and 'Pincher'?

8. What might the listener be given if she does as she's been told?

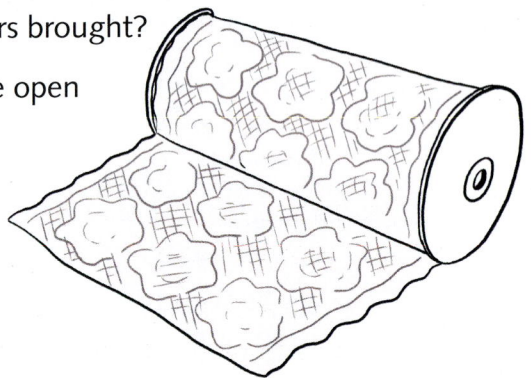

Try these

Write sentences to answer each question. Explain how or why you came up with your answer.

1. What do you think is meant by the line 'Them that asks no questions isn't told a lie'?

2. What do you think is meant by the line 'Watch the wall, my darling, while the Gentlemen go by'?

3. Why do you think 'King George's men' might be asking questions about the smugglers?

4. Even though the verse structure is not regular, the poet uses rhyming couplets. Why do you think he chose to do this?

5. Why do you think the house-dogs might follow the Gentlemen?

6. Who do you think the speaker of the poem could be?

7. What phrases from the poem helped you to reach this conclusion? Choose at least three.

8. In the context of the poem, do you think the smugglers are good or bad?

Now try these

1. Make a mind map about the different thoughts and feelings that the child listening to the poem would have, including what the child thinks of the Gentlemen before and after hearing the poem. Think about why the child would think or feel these different things.

2. Describe the character of the person speaking the poem based on what you learn from the extract.

3. Write a short announcement about the smugglers as if you are one of 'King George's men'.

4. Describe the rhythm of the poem in as much detail as possible. Do you think this is related to the content of the poem? If so, how?

5. Rewrite one or two verses of the poem using modern language.

Poetry: 'From a Railway Carriage'

Faster than fairies, faster than witches,
Bridges and houses, hedges and ditches;
And charging along like troops in a battle,
All through the meadows the horses and cattle;
All of the sights of the hill and the plain
Fly as thick as driving rain;
And ever again, in the wink of an eye,
Painted stations whistle by.

Here is a child who clambers and scrambles,
All by himself and gathering brambles;
Here is a tramp who stands and gazes;
And there is a green for stringing the daisies!
Here is a cart run away in the road
Lumping along with a man and a load;
And here is a mill and there is a river;
Each a glimpse and gone for ever!

Robert Louis Stevenson

Get started

Write sentences to answer each question. Refer to the poem in your answer.

1. In your own words, explain the vocabulary below in the context of the poem. Use a dictionary for help.

ditches	charging	driving	clambers	brambles	glimpse

2. According to the poem, what things are flying 'as thick as driving rain'?

3. According to the poem, what things are 'charging along like troops in a battle'?

4. How are the train stations described as moving?

5. What is the child doing?

6. What is the tramp doing?

7. How are the man and cart described as moving?

8. How many times in the poem is the word 'and' used?

Try these

Write sentences to answer each question. Explain how or why you came up with your answer.

1. What impressions does the poem give the reader about the train?

2. Why do you think the poet refers to 'fairies' and 'witches' in a poem about the railway?

3. Why do you think the tramp is gazing at the train?

4. Why does the poet say that the bridges, houses, hedges and ditches are moving?

5. Why do you think the word 'and' is used so frequently?

6. At what speed do you think the poem is meant to be read?

7. What do you think is meant by 'each a glimpse and gone for ever'?

8. This poem was written in 1885, when the railway industry was booming. How might this have influenced the poem?

Now try these

1. Read the poem out loud and practise until you can say it quickly. How does the poem sound?

2. How has the poet created this effect?

3. Find two similes in the poem. What effects do they create?

4. How do you think the child gathering brambles might feel about seeing the train? He may never have seen a train before. Note down two rhyming couplets about the train from this child's point of view.

5. Choose one of the sights glimpsed from the railway carriage and write a detailed description of it.

Non-fiction (instructions): 'Magic matchsticks'

Magic matchsticks

We are all intrigued by magicians, who seem to be able to perform impossible acts, such as pulling white rabbits out of hats and cutting a woman in half. Like all performances, though, a magician's real secret is in rehearsing thoroughly before showing anyone their tricks.

Here is a trick for you to learn. After you have practised thoroughly, try it on your family.

You will need

- several matchsticks
- a handkerchief with hems along the edges

What to do

1. Show the audience a matchstick.

2. Take a clean cotton handkerchief from your pocket, and shake it out, showing both sides to prove you are not hiding anything.

3. Wrap the matchstick in the handkerchief.

4. Ask one of the audience members to feel the matchstick inside the handkerchief, and to break it.

5. Shake the handkerchief, allowing the unbroken matchstick to fall onto the floor!

The secret

Before you begin the performance, slip a matchstick into the hem of the handkerchief. When you ask someone to break the wrapped-up matchstick, make sure that they break the one hidden in the hem (when they feel it, they will think it is the one they saw you wrap into the handkerchief).

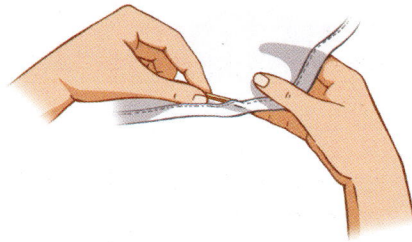

It's a good idea to have two or three handkerchiefs with matchsticks already secretly in the hems, as your audience is bound to be flabbergasted and ask you to do the trick again. But don't let them realise that you are changing handkerchiefs, or they may become suspicious!

Get started

Write sentences to answer each question. Refer to the instructions for your answer.

1. Explain the key vocabulary of this extract in your own words by rewriting the sentences below. Make sure you replace all of the underlined words. Use a dictionary for help.

> Put a <u>matchstick</u> into the <u>hem</u> of a <u>handkerchief</u>. <u>Rehearse</u> the trick <u>thoroughly</u>. Your friends will be <u>flabbergasted</u>, if they don't become <u>suspicious</u> of you!

2. What will these instructions help the reader to do?

3. What items do you need to perform the trick?

4. What is a magician's real secret?

5. What should you do before trying out the trick on your family?

6. What is Step 1 of the numbered instructions?

7. What is the secret of the trick?

8. What do you need to prepare before performing the trick, to set it up?

Try these

Write sentences to answer each question. Explain how or why you came up with your answer.

1. Is it important to shake out the handkerchief when you take it out of your pocket?

2. Is it really important to rehearse thoroughly?

3. How could the trick go wrong?

4. Why is it a good idea to have several handkerchiefs?

5. Why do you think people might be 'flabbergasted'?

6. Why might people get suspicious if they see you changing handkerchiefs?

7. Are these effective instructions?

8. How might you improve the instructions?

Now try these

1. Imagine you were in the audience, watching the trick for the first time. Write a few sentences to explain what you would think of the trick.

2. Describe the layout of these instructions.

3. Rewrite the instructions so that everything you need to do, including the set-up, is part of the numbered list in the order it needs to be done.

4. Write numbered instructions only for how to play your favourite game. You do not need to include any extra sections.

5. Write notes to explain to someone else how they can write effective instructions about how to make a packed lunch. What sections and other features will they need to include?

Non-fiction (historical): 'The Trojan War'

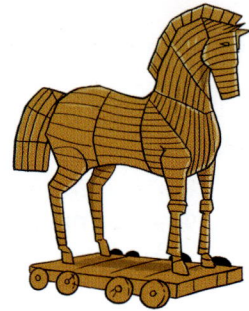

Troy was one of the greatest cities in the ancient world. It was surrounded by mighty walls, so huge they were considered impenetrable.

One day a Trojan prince called Paris travelled to Greece to meet the king, Menelaus, and Helen, his wife, who was undoubtedly the most beautiful woman he had ever set eyes on. Paris fell deeply in love with her and asked her to return to Troy with him. Initially Helen refused, but eventually Paris persuaded her, and they secretly eloped while Menelaus was away.

It is not difficult to imagine the king's bewilderment and anger when he returned. He sent his messengers to ask the Trojans to ensure the immediate return of Helen to Greece. When they refused, he brought together his best ships and bravest soldiers under the command of Agamemnon, his brother. It was thus that the Trojan War started.

Achilles

Legend has it that one of the great Greek heroes of the Trojan War was Achilles, a half-god, being the son of Zeus, the Greeks' most important god.

When he was a baby, Achilles' mother had dipped him in the magic waters of the Styx River. This meant every part of his body was thus protected from harm, except the heel by which his mother had held him when she dangled him in the waters. Achilles grew to become a strong, powerful soldier who could fight any battle, and without fear of ever being wounded!

One such battle led to the death of Paris's younger brother, Hector, but eventually Paris brought his revenge. One day, when Achilles was kneeling at prayer, Paris shot a poisoned arrow into his heel, killing the hitherto invincible hero. To this day, people talk of someone's Achilles heel, meaning his or her weak point.

The Trojan Horse

Neither side seemed to be getting the upper hand in the conflict. In desperation, the Greek hero Odysseus devised a plan to build a huge wooden statue of a horse and leave it as a religious offering. Unbeknown to the Trojans, Greek warriors hid inside the hollow statue. The other Greeks sailed away from Troy.

Delighted with the apparent retreat of their enemy, the Trojans opened the gates and flocked out of their city. As they were celebrating they came across the horse. Intrigued, they poked it and tapped it, and then found Sinon, a Greek soldier, hiding nearby.

They forced him, or so they thought, to divulge the secret of the horse. Sinon said that if the Trojans 'captured' the horse, the Greeks would be so demoralised they would never return to Troy again.

That night there was a great celebration in Troy with feasts and dancing, and lots of liquor! Later, with everyone exhausted and sleeping soundly, Sinon crept up to the huge horse and released the Greek soldiers. Then he opened the city gates to let in the other Greek soldiers, whose boats had returned under the cover of dark.

It was a rout! The Greeks destroyed the Trojan army before it could properly gather itself, and set fire to the city. Helen was forced to return to King Menelaus, and the long, bloody, Trojan War ended.

Get started

Write sentences to answer each question. Refer to the text in your answer.

1. What was Troy?

2. Why was Troy considered impenetrable?

3. Who was Paris?

4. Who was the most beautiful woman Paris had ever seen?

5. What was the first thing King Menelaus did when he found out Helen was gone?

6. Who was Achilles and why was he special?

7. How was Achilles killed?

8. Whose idea was the Trojan horse?

Try these

Write sentences to answer each question. Explain how or why you got your answer.

1. What kind of language is used in the extract? What effect does this have?

2. The extract is a historical recount. Do you think the story of the Trojan horse is true?

3. Do you think the story of Achilles is true?

4. Why did Sinon lie to the Trojans?

5. How do you think the Trojans felt when they first found the wooden horse?

6. How do you think Helen felt when she was forced to return to King Menelaus?

7. What do you think about the way the Greeks won the war?

8. Who do you think is the greatest hero in the extract?

Now try these

1. The extract uses some unusual and old-fashioned language. Choose more common modern words or phrases that could be swapped for the vocabulary below. Use a dictionary for help.

impenetrable	eloped	bewilderment	thus	hitherto
invincible	devised	unbeknown	flocked	intrigued
divulge	demoralised	rout		

2. Describe the character of Paris, based on what you learn in the extract.

3. Write notes about the different feelings that King Menelaus would have at different points during the story. When and why would he feel these different emotions?

4. Describe in your own words how the Trojans were finally defeated.

5. Write a dialogue between Paris and Helen when he is trying to persuade her to leave with him.

Fiction (legend): 'Shen Nung'

China's age of the 'Great Ten' was when each of ten successive emperors brought new skills and knowledge to this great civilisation, but none more so than Shen Nung. Some legends say he had the head of an ox, but the body of a man. Being part ox led him to invent the plough, which in China was always pulled by oxen. He showed his people how then to sow seed and cultivate crops.

He also taught them how to tame the forests and turn thickly overgrown woodlands into productive land. If they felled the trees in a small area and burned the stumps, they could plant their crops more easily. The ash would enrich the soil, helping their crops to grow well.

Shen Nung is also remembered as the god of medicine. He showed the people which plants would heal them when they were sick. According to the stories he was said to have a see-through stomach which enabled him to watch what was happening inside his body as he ate strange plants. One day he boiled some rare leaves and made a sort of vegetable stew. He drank the juice he strained from the mix. He had discovered tea!

Another of his useful discoveries was ginseng, a plant whose roots clean the blood of any impurities. It was soon recognised as a tonic, making tired people feel energetic and older people feel younger.

Sadly, Shen Nung grew careless and eventually died after swallowing a strange form of grass that was so sharp it cut his stomach to ribbons. But by then the great Emperor had discovered and invented so much his reputation was certain to live on for generations to come.

But so too was Shen Nung's wife to be remembered. She had mastered the art of breeding silkworms. This is a skill known as sericulture. Silkworms produce a thread that can be woven into silk cloth, for which the Chinese have ever since been renowned. To this day much of the best silk in the world comes from China. Shen Nung's wife was also deified, and became the goddess of housecrafts.

Medicine, tea, farming and fine cloth helped make China into one of the greatest civilisations the world has known – and dating back from a time several thousands of years ago, when people in most Western countries were still living in very primitive conditions.

Get started

Write sentences to answer each question. Refer to the legend in your answer.

1. In your own words, explain the vocabulary below in the context of the extract. Use a dictionary for help.

civilisation	plough	ox	cultivate	strained
impurities	renowned	deified	primitive	

2. What was China's age of the 'Great Ten'?

3. How did some legends describe Shen Nung's head?

4. How did Shen Nung teach his people to create productive land?

5. Shen Nung became remembered as a god. Of what was he the god?

6. According to the extract, what is ginseng?

7. According to the legend, how did Shen Nung die?

8. For what is Shen Nung's wife remembered?

Try these

Write sentences to answer each question. Explain how or why you came up with your answer.

1. How much do you think the discoveries made by Shen Nung and his wife influenced China's success as a country?

2. Did the discoveries of Shen Nung and his wife make people's lives better?

3. Why was it important for the Chinese people to grow their crops well?

4. Do you think all of the information about Shen Nung is untrue?

5. Why do you think legends might mix truth with stories?

6. What is the effect of the untrue information?

7. Why was having the head of an ox appropriate for Shen Nung?

8. Based on what you learn in the extract, why do you think someone might be deified?

Now try these

1. Make a mind map about the different skills and knowledge that Shen Nung brought to China. Include details about how these things influence life then and now.

2. Explain how the discoveries made by Shen Nung and his wife have affected your life in the modern world.

3. Imagine you could talk to Shen Nung. Plan six questions you would like to ask him. What would you like to find out about his life and discoveries?

4. Write a dialogue between Shen Nung and his people as he explains one of his discoveries to them.

5. Write a diary entry as Shen Nung after he has discovered ginseng. What parts of his life will Shen Nung mention in his diary? How might he refer to the parts of his story that you believe are untrue?

Non-fiction (information text): 'Your Brain'

From 'Your Brain' by Sally Morgan

The control centre

Your brain is the control centre of your body. It works 24 hours a day, seven days a week for the whole of your life, even when you're sleeping.

Controls and checks

Your brain controls everything that's going on in your body. It makes lots of checks too, to be certain that all is working properly. It tells you when you're hungry, tired or in pain. It makes sure that you breathe and that your heart keeps pumping. It's also the place where you do all your thinking and store your memories.

Our brain is the most advanced in the animal kingdom. It allows us to do things many other animals can't, such as read, write and learn languages.

Many cells

Your brain is found inside your head. It's a surprisingly large organ. An adult's brain weighs about 1.4 kilograms. It's very soft and pinky-white on the outside and grey-white inside.

Your brain is made up of billions of cells. Cells are the tiniest part of your body, so small that you can't see them. There are many different types of cell in your body, each designed to do a particular job. For example, there are red blood cells that carry oxygen around your body, bone cells that make up your bones, skin cells that form a covering for your body and liver cells that make bile, a liquid that helps to break down your food.

There is fat and water in your brain too, but no blood. Instead, your brain is surrounded by blood vessels. Blood flows around your body in blood vessels. The blood brings food and oxygen to your brain.

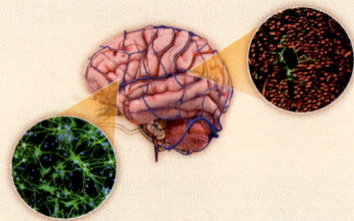

Large head

Newborn babies have large heads for their size. This is because they are born with brains that are almost full size. As they get older, their body grows, so their head does not look as large.

Get started

Write sentences to answer each question. Refer to the text in your answer.

1. What role does the extract say your brain plays in your body?
2. When does your brain work?
3. What does your brain control?
4. What does the extract say we can do but other animals can't?
5. Where is your brain found?
6. How much does an adult's brain weigh?
7. What does a brain look like?
8. What is your brain made up of?

Try these

Write sentences to answer each question. Explain how or why you came up with your answer.

1. This is a factual information text. Are there any examples of opinion in the text?
2. What kind of language is used in the extract? What effect does this have?
3. Why is the photograph of the newborn baby useful for the reader?
4. Which fact from the extract surprises or interests you the most?
5. Why do you think readers would want to read this text?
6. Do you think it is important for humans to understand the way our bodies work? Why do you think this?
7. How do you think the author knows that the facts in the text are true?
8. What doesn't the extract tell you about your brain?

Now try these

1. Create a glossary for this text that could go into the non-fiction book 'Your Brain'. Use a dictionary for help if you need to.
2. In your own words, describe the structure and features of this information text extract.
3. Explain why subheadings have been used in the text.
4. Based on the information in the extract, design a leaflet or a poster meant to encourage people to value their brains. You could encourage them to look after their brains by eating healthily and using bicycle helmets.
5. Create a presentation about 'Your Brain' that you should show to your class.

Non-fiction (biography): 'Barack Obama'

Barack Hussein Obama was born on 4 August 1961, in Honolulu, Hawaii. Obama's mother, Ann Dunham, grew up in Kansas, USA, and his father, Barack Obama Sr, was born in Nyanza Province, Kenya. They met at the University of Hawaii and married on 2 February 1961.

Obama's parents separated when he was only two years old, and later divorced. Obama Sr went on to Harvard University to pursue further studies, and then returned to Kenya in 1965. In 1966, Barack's mother married Lolo Soetoro and the family moved to Indonesia. Several incidents in Indonesia left Barack's mother afraid for her son's safety and education so, at the age of ten, he was sent back to Hawaii to live with his maternal grandparents. His mother and half-sister later joined them.

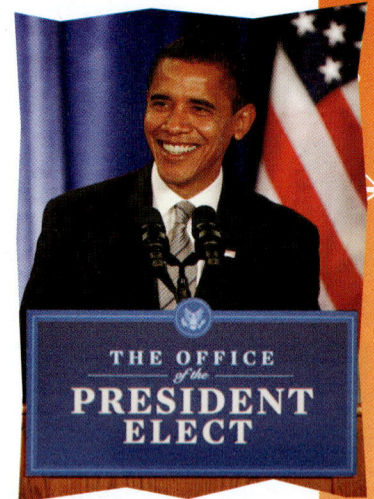

While living with his grandparents, Obama was given a place in the highly regarded Punahou Academy, where he excelled in basketball. As one of only three black students at the school, Obama became conscious of racism and what it meant to be African-American. He later described how he struggled to reconcile other people's perceptions of his multiracial heritage with his own sense of himself.

"I began to notice there was nobody like me in the Christmas catalogues … and that Santa was a white man," he said.

Obama was also unhappy because of the absence of his father. His father wrote to him regularly but, though he travelled around the world on official business for Kenya, he only visited once. Obama Jr was 22 years old when he received the news that his father had died in a car accident in Kenya.

Obama attended Columbia University and found New York's racial tension inescapable. He attended Harvard Law School and chose to practise civil rights law in Chicago. He represented victims of housing and employment discrimination and worked on voting rights legislation. He married Michelle Robinson, a fellow attorney. Eventually he was elected to the Illinois State Senate. His district included some of the poorest ghettos on the South Side.

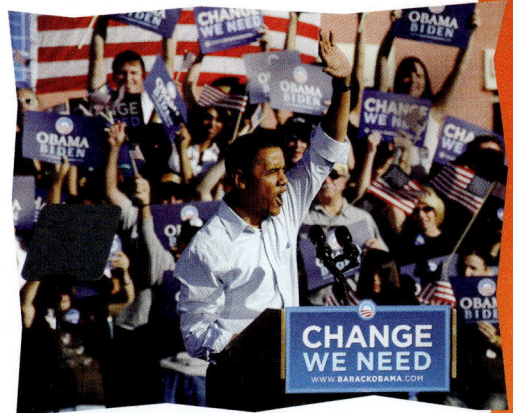

In 2004, Obama was elected to the US Senate as a Democrat. He gained national attention by giving a rousing and well-received speech at the Democratic National Convention. In 2008 he ran for President and won. In January 2009, he was sworn in as the 44th President of the United States, the first African-American ever elected to that position.

Get started

Write sentences to answer each question. Refer to the biography in your answer.

1. What is Barack Obama's date of birth?

2. Where was he born?

3. Where did he live when he was between five and ten years old?

4. In which sport did he excel?

5. What did Obama notice about the Christmas catalogues?

6. What was the bad news that he received when he was 22 years old?

7. In which year was he elected to the US Senate as a Democrat?

8. What happened in January 2009?

Try these

Write sentences to answer each question. Explain how or why you came up with your answer.

1. The extract is a biography. What do you think a biography is?

2. What features of a biography can you find in this extract?

3. Why might people be interested to read the biography of Barack Obama?

4. What is meant by the terms 'racism' and 'African-American'?

5. What is the effect of the one quote used in the extract?

6. How do you think Obama felt when he looked at the Christmas catalogues?

7. How do you think his mother felt when she sent him to live with his grandparents?

8. Which part of Barack's life do you most admire?

Now try these

1. Write notes about the different feelings that Barack Obama's mother may have had at different points during the story. When and why would she feel these different emotions?

2. Describe the character of Barack Obama based on what you learn in the extract.

3. Imagine you could interview Obama. Plan six interesting or unusual questions you would like to ask him. What would you like to find out in order to understand his life better?

4. Write a set of interview questions that you would need to ask someone if you were preparing to write their biography.

5. Explain why you think Obama wanted to practise civil rights law. Use a dictionary or the internet for help if you need to.

Fiction (modern): 'The Hedgehog Mystery'

From 'The Hedgehog Mystery' by Ally Kennen

Chapter 1

I don't know anyone else with a gran like mine. For one thing, she rides an enormous motorbike. It's a BSA Road Rocket and it's jet black with orange flames painted down the sides. It goes like stink. Gran calls it "Fenella" and we hear them coming a mile off. Gran lives in the house over the road from mine where she keeps the bike chained up in her front garden. Gran has a leather jacket with a hedgehog painted on the back. She wears lots of silver rings and her hair's dyed red. But she's not scary; she's anything but. Gran's the softest old bird ever. She's part of a gang called the "Hedgehogs". They're all women and they all ride powerful motorbikes. They're also all over 50.

Mum shakes her head in despair when she hears Gran roaring down the street. "Sixty-two year old grandmothers shouldn't ride motorbikes," she says. Mum's like that. She's full of shoulds and shouldn'ts, dos and don'ts. She can be a right pain. Gran says it's because she loves us so much, she's only trying to look after us. But I get annoyed with Mum sometimes. She thinks the whole world's a big, scary, dangerous place where everyone and everything's out to get you. And one day, horribly, she turns out to be right.

Every day, after school, me and my brother Morris go to Gran's. She gives us our tea and looks after us until Mum comes home from work.

I follow Morris through Gran's front gate. My brother's nine – one year younger than me. He likes making cakes, sleeping and watching telly. He's big for his age, and calmer than me.

I take my key out of my purse and let us in.

"I'm in the living room," calls Gran.

Morris and I kick off our school shoes and close the door. He heads straight for the kitchen and I find Gran in the front room.

She's standing on her head on a bright pink cushion.

Get started

Write sentences to answer each question. Refer to the text in your answer.

1. What does Gran's motorbike look like?

2. What does Gran call her motorbike?

3. Where does Gran keep her motorbike?

4. What does Gran look like?

5. Why does Gran have a hedgehog painted on the back of her jacket?

6. What is Mum's opinion of Gran's motorbike?

7. How does Gran defend Mum's behaviour?

8. Who is Morris?

Try these

Write sentences to answer each question. Explain how or why you came up with your answer.

1. What do you think the phrase 'goes like stink' means?

2. Why do you think Mum is disapproving of Gran's behaviour?

3. Which sentence warns the reader that something bad is going to happen in the story?

4. Is the narrator still annoyed by her mother?

5. What part does Gran play in the family's life?

6. Why do you think Gran was standing on her head?

7. How do you think the narrator feels about her Gran?

8. Do you think this is a historical or a modern story?

Now try these

1. Describe the character of Gran based on what you learn in the extract.

2. How does this extract from the beginning of the story help you as a reader to engage quickly with the story and the characters?

3. Make a mind map about the different feelings the speaker would have at different points during the extract as she describes Gran, and then Mum, and then the after-school routine.

4. Explain how the sentence 'Every day, after school, me and my brother Morris go to Gran's' marks a change in the story.

5. Write the next part of the story. What will Gran say? What horrible thing might happen to prove Mum right?

Fiction (traditional tale): 'The Dragon Pearl'

From 'Two Dragon Tales' by Dawn Casey

Now Xiao Sheng and his mother had plenty of everything. And what they had, they shared. The people of the village had always been good to Xiao Sheng and his mother, and now Xiao Sheng made sure everyone was provided for. Though the rains didn't fall and the crops didn't grow, everyone had enough to eat. Life was good, for a while…

Bang! Bang! Bang!

Xiao Sheng's mother looked up in alarm. "Who's that hammering on the door?" But before Xiao Sheng could answer, the door burst open and in strode their landlord, Lord Zhou.

"I know you have a magic pearl," he shouted. "All the land around here belongs to ME. Whatever comes from the land belongs to ME. That pearl is MINE. Give it to me!"

Xiao Sheng's mother went pale with fear, but Xiao Sheng darted to the rice jar and grabbed the pearl from its hiding place. "It's a dragon's pearl," he said. "It's not yours or mine to keep. Its gifts belong to everyone."

"How dare you!" Lord Zhou roared, and he lunged towards Xiao Sheng, to snatch the pearl away.

Without a moment's thought, Xiao Sheng put the pearl in his mouth. Lord Zhou grabbed his shoulders and shook him hard. "Spit it out! It's MINE!"

"I can't." Xiao Sheng looked at his mother with wide eyes. "I've swallowed it."

Suddenly, Xiao Sheng's face flushed red. The pearl felt like a ball of fire burning in his belly. "What's happening?" he cried.

Xiao Sheng rushed to the water jug and gulped down every drop of water. He drained all the tea in the pot. Then he ran outside and began to drink the muddy trickle of water from the river bed.

And as he drank, his body began to change. Swirling steam poured from his nostrils. Brilliant scales rippled down his back. Magnificent antlers sprouted through his hair.

Xiao Sheng was a dragon.

Throwing back his mighty head, he whirled into the sky and blew out cloud after billowing cloud.

Get started

Write sentences to answer each question. Refer to the text in your answer.

1. Who now had plenty of everything?

2. Who was banging on the door?

3. What magic item did Xiao Sheng have?

4. Why did Xiao Sheng's mother go pale?

5. What did Xiao Sheng do to hide the pearl?

6. How did the pearl feel in Xiao Sheng's belly?

7. What did Xiao Sheng do with the tea in the pot?

8. What happened to Xiao Sheng's body?

Try these

Write sentences to answer each question. Explain how or why you came up with your answer.

1. What clues are there that this extract is from the middle of the story, rather than its beginning or end?

2. Why did Xiao Sheng make sure everyone in the village was provided for?

3. If it weren't for Xiao Sheng, why wouldn't the villagers have enough to eat?

4. Why do you think Xiao Sheng and his mother had plenty of everything? Do you think they had always had plenty of everything?

5. How do you think Xiao Sheng felt about Lord Zhou?

6. How do you think Xiao Sheng's mother felt about her son?

7. Which words does the author use to suggest that Xiao Sheng's transformation is beautiful rather than horrific?

8. Who do you think the pearl belonged to?

Now try these

1. Describe the character of Xiao Sheng based on what you learn in the extract.

2. Make a mind map about the different feelings that Xiao Sheng's mother would have had at different points during the story, including before and during the encounter with Lord Zhou. Think about when and why she would feel these different emotions.

3. What evidence is there in the text that Xiao Sheng didn't mean to swallow the pearl?

4. How do you think Xiao Sheng feels about turning into a dragon?

5. Write the next part of the story. What will Xiao Sheng the dragon do? How do you think his transformation might be able to help the people of the village?

Poetry: 'What on Earth?' and 'Progress Man!'

From 'Caliban's Cave' by Judith Nicholls

What on Earth?

What on earth are we doing?
Once wood-pigeons flew,
and young badgers tunnelled
where oak and ash grew …

Now the forest's a runway,
and all that flies through
is a whining grey plane
where the pigeons once flew.

Where on earth are we going?
At the end of the lane
once blackberries hung
in soft autumn rain …

Now the lane is a car park,
and never again
will fruit fill our baskets
down in the lane.

Why on earth are we crying?
Once morning dew shone
on hawthorn and primrose
caught in the sun …

Now the forest is carpeted
only with stone.
No primrose, no hawthorn:
the forest has gone.

Progress Man!

Hurry now! *cried Progress*,
just see what I can do!
Watch my chain saw, feel my axe;
my ways are great for you,

'cos I'm a swinging, singing,
racing, chasing, do-it-how-I-can,
I'm the swinging, singing,
racing, chasing Progress Man!

See me chop your forests down,
we need a motorway!
You have some roads already …?
Well, not enough, I say,

and I'm a swinging, singing,
racing, chasing, do-it-how-I-can,
I'm the swinging, singing,
racing, chasing Progress Man!

What's a little drop of oil
spilt over golden sand?
It's just a tiny price to pay,
the world has so much land,

and I'm a swinging, singing,
racing, chasing, do-it-how-I-can,
I'm the swinging, singing,
racing, chasing Progress Man!

Get started

Write sentences to answer each question. Refer to the poems in your answer.

1. What flew where oak and ash grew?

2. What flies through the forest now?

3. Where did blackberries once hang?

4. What has the lane become?

5. What does Progress Man say we need?

6. What is Progress Man's response to being told that we have some roads already?

7. What does Progress Man say is a tiny price to pay?

8. How much land does Progress Man say the world has?

Try these

Write sentences to answer each question. Explain how or why you came up with your answer.

1. What message is the poet trying to convey in 'What on Earth'?

2. What message is the poet trying to convey in 'Progress Man!'?

3. Who is the speaker in 'Progress Man!'?

4. Who is the 'we' mentioned in both poems?

5. How are the rhyming patterns similar in the two poems?

6. Do you think the line 'the forest's a runway' is a metaphor, or is it meant literally?

7. Find one example of personification. If you are unsure what personification is, look it up in a dictionary or ask your teacher.

8. Which poem do you prefer? Why?

Now try these

1. In your own words, describe how the poems are similar to one another.

2. In your own words, describe how the poems are different from one another.

3. Describe the character of 'Progress Man' based on what you learn in the poem.

4. Look up the word 'progress' in the dictionary and write down its definition. Do you think 'Progress Man' is an actual man? If not, what is it? Why do you think this?

5. Write two verses in a similar style to 'What on Earth?' based on your views about protecting the environment. Use the same rhyming pattern.

Non-fiction (information text): 'How to be an Ancient Greek in 25 easy stages'

From 'How to be an Ancient Greek in 25 easy stages' by Scoular Anderson

Stage 3: Go from riches to rags

If you were a Mycenaean king or queen who had just died, you were buried in a tomb with large amounts of gold and jewellery. The Mycenaeans were wealthy people but they were also warlike. A king's weapons, armour and shield were buried with him as well.

Objects found in Mycenaean graves

gold mask placed over the face of → a dead king

bronze suit of armour

↖ shields

pot painted with an octopus design

The little kingdoms that made up Ancient Greece were often at war with one another. In the centre of each kingdom was a polis (city). So that it could be defended from attack, a city was surrounded by a thick, high wall and often situated on top of a rock, when it was known as an acropolis (high city).

Mycenae was one of the most important Mycenaean high cities. Its walls were made of enormous blocks of stone and there were statues of lions above the main gate.

The Mycenaean civilisation only lasted a few hundred years. Like the Minoans, the Mycenaeans ran into trouble beyond their control. There was a long period of bad weather which led to poor harvests and starvation. Many Mycenaeans migrated to other lands and left their cities to crumble.

If you were one of those who stayed behind, you probably scratched a living on a small farm. Nothing much else happened for a long time and the Greeks even forgot how to read and write. These times became known as the Dark Ages. It was two hundred years before the Ancient Greeks got their act together again.

Stage 4: Make your voice heard

One of the most powerful cities in Ancient Greece was Athens. The Acropolis of Athens was once a fortified city on a rocky hill but, over time, the city moved downhill leaving the top of the hill as a sacred place filled only with temples.

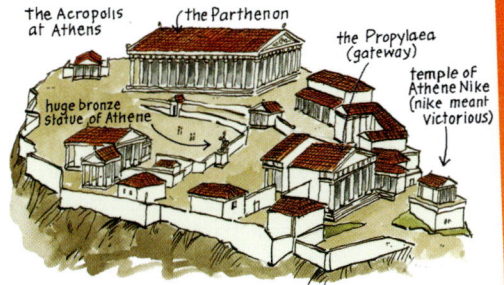

The biggest of these was the Parthenon which was the temple of the goddess Athene who gave her name to the city.

The Athenians were cultured people who liked music, poetry and the theatre. However, they were often at war with other cities and so they kept a fleet of fighting ships in the nearby port of Piraeus.

Get started

Write sentences to answer each question. Refer to the information text in your answer.

1. If you were a Mycenaean king who had just died, what would you be buried with?

2. How are the Mycenaean people described?

3. What four objects does the image tell you were found in Mycenaean graves?

4. What was in the centre of each kingdom in Ancient Greece?

5. What does the word 'acropolis' mean?

6. How long did the Mycenaean civilisation last?

7. What did the Greeks forget how to do during the Dark Ages?

8. According to the extract, who was Athene?

Try these

Write sentences to answer each question. Explain how or why you came up with your answer.

1. Why did the Mycenaeans leave their cities to crumble?

2. Why do you think the city of Athens moved downhill?

3. What information does the image of Athens give the reader?

4. Which fact from the extract surprises or interests you the most?

5. Why may readers want to read this text?

6. Do you think it is important for us to understand about people and culture from history? Why do you think this?

7. Do you think you would have liked to live in ancient Athens? Why do you think this?

8. How do you think the author knows that the facts in the text are true?

Now try these

1. Create a glossary for this text that could go into the non-fiction book 'How to be an Ancient Greek in 25 easy stages'. Use a dictionary for help if you need to.

2. In your own words, describe the structure and features of this information text extract.

3. Explain why the author has split up the text into '25 easy stages'.

4. Based on the information in the extract, design a leaflet or a poster that could encourage other Ancient Greek people to visit the polis of Athens.

5. Create a presentation about Ancient Greek cities that you could show to your class.

Non-fiction (autobiography): 'Ade Adepitan: A Paralympian's Story'

From 'Ade Adepitan: A Paralympian's Story' by Ade Adepitan

The Newham Rollers

I didn't get into basketball until I was about 12 or 13 years old. There was a disabled school in the area, where they'd set up a sports club and within that a wheelchair basketball team called the Newham Rollers. At first I didn't want to join. For a start, I didn't really think of myself as being disabled, plus I had a perception of wheelchairs as ugly, clunky things that said more about you than helped you.

But in the end I went along and at the games I saw some of the guys from the GB basketball team, who happened to be training. I was amazed by the chairs they were using – state-of-the-art funky wheelchairs – and they were flying up and down the court, doing wheelies and all sorts. The players were all really big, with massive arms – they looked like athletes and were so cool. As they were going past, one of them gave me a wink and I thought, that's it, that's what I want to be – I want to be like these guys. I was getting frustrated at school playing football, because as everyone else was getting bigger it was harder and harder for me to compete with them, so I decided to try wheelchair basketball instead.

When I got in the chair, which I had to borrow from the club, I was so small that it felt like the basketball was the same size as me. I remember throwing it up to the net for the first time and it didn't even get close! I played in the junior championships anyway, but, surprise, surprise, we lost.

I had a strong sense of pride and wasn't used to losing. During the next year I practised really hard. I spent hours working on my hand-eye co-ordination, sitting on the floor at home throwing a ball at the living room wall and catching it. I also got my own wheelchair. When we went back to that tournament the next year, we reached the final.

Get started

Write sentences to answer each question. Refer to the text in your answer.

1. How old was Ade when he started playing basketball?

2. What was his first wheelchair basketball team called?

3. How does Ade describe the GB players?

4. What was different about their wheelchairs, compared to regular wheelchairs?

5. At what precise moment did Ade decide he wanted to be like the GB basketball team players?

6. How did Ade feel when he first sat in the basketball wheelchair?

7. What happened when Ade first played in the junior championships?

8. What happened when Ade returned to the tournament the following year?

Try these

Write sentences to answer each question. Explain how or why you came up with your answer.

1. The extract is an autobiography. What do you think an autobiography is?

2. What features of an autobiography can you find in this extract?

3. Why might people be interested in reading the autobiography of Ade Adepitan?

4. Why do you think Ade might have such a strong sense of pride?

5. Before getting a basketball wheelchair, Ade was having therapy to help him to walk. How do you think this might help to explain how he felt about wheelchairs?

6. How do you think his parents may have felt about him starting to use a wheelchair?

7. How did Ade's perception of wheelchairs change during the time described in the extract?

8. Which part of Ade's experiences do you most admire?

Now try these

1. Write notes about the different impressions that Ade's school friends may have had at different points during the extract. When and why would they think these different things?

2. Describe the character of Ade Adepitan based on what you learn in the extract.

3. Imagine you could interview Ade Adepitan. Plan six interesting or unusual questions you would like to ask him. What would you like to find out in order to understand his life better?

4. Write a set of guiding questions that you would need to ask yourself if you were preparing to write your own autobiography.

5. In your own words, explain why you think Ade Adepitan wanted to achieve sporting success.

Poetry: 'Summer Afternoon' and 'Gathering in the Days'

From 'Gathering in the Days' by Gareth Owen

Summer Afternoon

The mud cakes dry in the farmyard
The clouds have died a death
The tarmac shimmers like water
The air is holding its breath.

The dogs fall asleep to the humming
Of cruising bumblebees
And the cows stand still as statues
As the stream slides past their knees.

Gathering in the Days

I saw my grandad late last evening
On a hillside scything hay
Wiped his brow and gazed about him
Gathering in the day.

My grandmother beside the fireplace
Sleeps the afternoons away
Wakes and stirs the dying embers
Gathering in the day.

Heard screams of laughter from the orchard
Saw a boy and a girl at play
Watched them turn their heads towards me
Gathering in the day.

And my mother at a window
On some long-forgotten May
Lifts her eyes and smiles upon us
Gathering in the day.

And all the people I remember
Stopped their lives and glanced my way
Shared the selfsame sun an instant
Gathering in the day.

Get started

Write sentences to answer each question. Refer to the text in your answer.

1. What is happening to the mud cakes?
2. What has happened to the clouds?

3. What is the shimmering tarmac compared to?

4. What can the dogs hear that sends them to sleep?

5. Who was on the hillside scything hay?

6. What does the speaker's grandmother do in the afternoons?

7. Who was playing in the orchard?

8. What is the speaker's mother doing as she gathers in the day?

Try these

Write sentences to answer each question. Explain how or why you came up with your answer.

1. What is the weather like in 'Summer Afternoon'?

2. What is the weather like in 'Gathering in the Days'?

3. Why do you think the cows are standing still in the stream?

4. How are the rhyming patterns similar in the two poems?

5. How many beats are in the lines of the two poems?

6. Do you think the poet is trying to portray negative or positive emotions in these poems?

7. Find one example of personification.

8. What do you think the phrase 'gathering in the day' means?

Now try these

1. In your own words, describe how the poems are similar to one another.

2. In your own words, describe how the poems are different from one another.

3. Describe the character of the speaker of 'Gathering in the Days' based on what you learn in the poem.

4. Explain how the final verse of 'Gathering in the Days' draws the poem to a conclusion and unites all the other verses.

5. Write a poem similar to 'Summer Afternoon', entitled 'Autumn Morning'. Use the same number of lines and verses, and the same rhyming pattern.